Published by Charlesbridge
85 Main Street
Watertown, MA 02472
(617) 926-0329
www.charlesbridge.com

First published in France in 2015 by Éditions Rue du monde, 5 rue de Port-Royal, 78960
Voisins-le-Bretonneux, France, as *Malala: pur le droit des filles à l'éducation* by Raphaële
Frier and Aurélia Fronty. Copyright © 2015 Rue du monde · www.ruedumonde.fr

Library of Congress Cataloging-in-Publication Data
Names: Frier, Raphaële, 1970– author. | Fronty, Aurélia, illustrator.
Title: Malala: activist for girls' education/Raphaële Frier; illustrated
    by Aurélia Fronty.
Other titles: Malala. English
Description: 1st US edition. | Watertown, MA: Charlesbridge, 2017. |
    Translation of: Malala: pour le droit des filles à l'éducation.
Identifiers: LCCN 2016009136 (print) | LCCN 2016020768 (ebook) |
    ISBN 9781580897853 (reinforced for library use) | ISBN 9781632895912 (ebook) |
    ISBN 9781632895929 (ebook pdf)
Subjects: LCSH: Yousafzai, Malala, 1997—Juvenile literature. |
    Girls—Education—Pakistan—Juvenile literature. | Sex discrimination in
    education—Pakistan—Juvenile literature. | Women social
    reformers—Pakistan—Biography—Juvenile literature. | Political
    activists—Pakistan—Biography—Juvenile literature.
Classification: LCC LC2330 .F7513 2017 (print) | LCC LC2330 (ebook) | DDC
    370.82095491—dc23
LC record available at https://lccn.loc.gov/2016009136

Printed in China
(hc) 10 9 8 7 6 5 4 3 2 1

Display type set in ITC Officina Serif
Text type set in ITC Officina Serif and ITC Officina Sans
Printed by 1010 Printing International Limited in Huizhou, Guangdong, China
Production supervision by Brian G. Walker
Designed by Sarah Richards Taylor

MALALA
Activist for Girls' Education

Raphaële Frier

Illustrated by
Aurélia Fronty

i⌒i Charlesbridge

Malala is born at dawn in 1997. She is the first child of Ziauddin Yousafzai and Tor Pekai. They live in the large city of Mingora, which spreads out across the depths of the Swat Valley in Pakistan. Their home is across the street from a school for girls that Ziauddin founded—the Khushal School.

Malala's father is not sorry that his child is a girl, as some new fathers in their country might be. Ziauddin is very fond of his Pashtun people, but he is not as fond of some of their traditions.

Ziauddin asks friends and family to throw dried fruits, candies, and coins into her cradle, as they would for a boy.

Malala grows up with the smell of notebooks in the air. It doesn't take long for her first little brother to arrive. He is named Khushal, like his father's school.

The two children run together in the classrooms after school is over, or play hide-and-seek with neighbors. They fly kites on the rooftop and try to touch the sky.

Malala and Khushal look out at the city toward Mount Elum, where the snow never melts.

Malala loves her grandfather's village, way up in the mountains, far from the pollution in Mingora. There, the water in the lakes and waterfalls is pure, the nuts are abundant, and the honey is delicious. In the winter, people make snow bears.

But Malala does not love all the village stories, like the one about Shahida, who was sold to an old man for marriage. In the Pashtun mountains, even more than in the city, men are the ones who are visible in society and the workplace, while women stay at home and must obey the men. Most women, like Malala's mother, cannot read or write.

Malala likes to climb up on the roof at home in Mingora so she can listen to the sounds of the city, the chatter of the birds, and the words of her father talking about politics with his friends while they drink cardamom tea.

They talk about how the Taliban, a powerful and violent political group, has set another school on fire. Malala's father and his friends hate that the Taliban wants students to study strict, very conservative interpretations of the Qur'an.

They call the Taliban an ignorant group and worry that it will cause terrible problems.

Ziauddin often shares ideas with his daughter. Malala knows that she is lucky to have thoughtful parents. Her mother loves a Pashto song that goes like this:

Don't kill doves in the garden.

You kill one, and the others won't come.

Malala thinks about what this means.

A terrible earthquake shakes the region on October 8, 2005. The mountain villages are reduced to dust.

Soon afterward Malala realizes that her father is worried about something else, too. A man named Fazlullah, who is in charge of the nearby Taliban, scares Ziauddin. Fazlullah wants to close Ziauddin's school—his school for girls.

Fazlullah takes advantage of people's sadness about the earthquake. Time and time again, through his local radio station, he tells them that their sins caused the earthquake. He tells them to stop listening to music and watching movies. He says this will make everything better.

Malala's father is heartbroken. He rejects the use of religion to threaten freedom.

But people worry: What if Fazlullah is telling the truth?

Fear settles in the valley. Some people throw their televisions, computers, CDs, and other belongings into fires.

But the Taliban insists that even more needs to be done.

People stop dancing. Beauty parlors close. Men stop shaving because the Taliban requires that beards are worn. Women's bodies and faces are covered by burqas—long cloth garments that flow from head to toe. The Taliban is on patrol. Taliban members arrest people who disobey them and whip or kill people if they resist the new rules. Ziauddin is afraid, but he dares to disagree. He allows Malala to speak out against the Taliban in a September 2008 speech covered by newspapers and television stations. There she asks, "How dare the Taliban take away my basic right to education?" She is only eleven years old.

As 2008 ends, the Taliban announces another ban: girls no longer have the right to go to school as of January 15, 2009.

"How can they stop us from going to school?" Malala is upset.

Her friends are angry, too. "They have already blown up hundreds of schools, and no one has done anything."

Then an opportunity arrives. Malala is recruited to write about girls and education. Her first blog post, written under the pseudonym Gul Makai, appears on the British Broadcasting Corporation's website.

DIARY OF A PAKISTANI SCHOOLGIRL

Saturday, January 3, 2009

I Am Afraid

I had a terrible dream yesterday with military helicopters and the Taliban. . . .

Malala's words do not stop the Taliban. The group goes farther north and uses even more violence.

Soon there are peace agreements between the Pakistani government and the Taliban. But the agreements don't work in the end. The Taliban continues to use violence against the people. Then tanks and guns arrive in the valley.

It is war.

Malala and her family abandon their house and travel to the village where her grandparents live. They stay in four cities over three months before they can return home. Mingora is again in ruins. But the Taliban has been driven away.

Schools are rebuilt so everyone can study, even girls. Malala wants everyone to get an education.

Malala is elected speaker of the child assembly associated with the Khpal Kor Foundation, which promotes the rights of children. In this leadership role, she begins as a children's rights activist.

But soon the Taliban returns to the valley. Schools are destroyed again. Supporters of freedom are executed.

Malala doesn't get discouraged. Although she is not yet fourteen, she is already an important person in her country.

She continues to write her blog and fight for girls' right to an education. Malala is often invited to speak and receives lots of assistance for her campaign. The Pakistani government awards her the first-ever National Youth Peace Prize.

By 2011 Malala is so successful, she is able to create an educational foundation. It helps her and those who support her work.

But her family is threatened by the Taliban. The militant group does not like her father's schools or Malala's activism.

On October 9, 2012, Malala is riding home on the school bus. It stops suddenly.

A man shouts to the driver, "Is this the Khushal School bus?"

A second man enters the bus and yells, "Who is Malala?"

Nobody answers, but some students look at their friend. It is obvious who Malala is— she is the only one who has taken off her headscarf on the bus. One of the men shoots Malala three times.

Everyone screams.

Two other girls are hurt.

Malala slumps forward onto her best friend's lap. The bus driver speeds to the nearest hospital in Swat.

The Pakistani president, along with other politicians and famous Muslims, condemns the assassination attempt. The Taliban claims responsibility.

Malala is not doing well. Her father wishes out loud that he could take her place. The doctors and the government decide to accept an offer for Malala to be treated at a hospital in Birmingham, England. Malala must go alone, because it is too dangerous for her father to leave her mother and brothers alone in Pakistan.

She is confused when she awakes in England, but she speaks on the phone to her parents. Finally her family arrives. Letters and gifts are sent from all over the world.

After several operations and a lot of time to heal,
Malala takes classes in Birmingham. The Taliban doesn't
silence Malala. She keeps fighting for education rights.

There are more than five million children in Pakistan
who don't have the right to go to primary school. Most
of them are girls. Malala empathizes with young girls
in other countries—such as Afghanistan, Nigeria, and
Nepal—who live where education for girls isn't valued.

Many people believe that women should stay at home to watch the younger children, cook, do housework, and get water from the wells.

Girls are often required to marry at a very young age. Many families believe that only boys should have jobs.

Malala disagrees with all these ideas.

On Malala's sixteenth birthday, July 12, 2013, hundreds of people from around the world hear her speak at the United Nations in New York City. Malala wears a shawl that belonged to Benazir Bhutto, a Pakistani prime minister who was assassinated.

I am here to speak up for the right of education of every child. I want education for the sons and daughters of the Taliban and all the terrorists and extremists.

She speaks about Martin Luther King Jr., Nelson Mandela, and Mahatma Gandhi.

Poverty, ignorance, injustice, racism, and the deprivation of basic rights are the main problems faced by both men and women.

She speaks about women's rights and girls' education.

There was a time when women social activists asked men to stand up for their rights. But this time we will do it by ourselves.

Malala puts hope in hearts and tears in eyes.

One child, one teacher, one pen, and one book can change the world.

The next year, Malala receives the Nobel Peace Prize. At seventeen, she is the youngest person ever to receive the prestigious award.

But the beautiful Swat Valley where pomegranate and
fig trees bloom still isn't free. Malala and her family
can't go home because they are under death threats.
Weapons still rule. Shots ring out, along with bombs
from drones.

Fighting results in victims on both sides—sometimes
innocent victims. Malala talks with the president of the
United States about the situation, with the hope that
peace will triumph quickly in Pakistan.

Malala dreams of books and notebooks
instead of war in her beloved valley.

The Nobel Peace Prize gives
Malala wings. She visits Syrian
refugee camps in Lebanon,
she supports school projects
in Nigeria, and more.

Malala has been known worldwide ever since the United Nations designated July 12, 2013, her sixteenth birthday, as Malala Day. The day celebrates that every child should have the right to go to school, to learn to write and count, and to know the happiness of reading. Freely.

Malala Yousafzai
Learning Is a Universal Right

"Dear sisters and brothers, we realize the importance of light when we see darkness. We realize the importance of our voice when we are silenced. In the same way, when we were in Swat, the north of Pakistan, we realized the importance of pens and books when we saw the guns."

—Excerpt from Malala Yousafzai's speech to the United Nations in New York on July 12, 2013

"I dedicate this award to all those children who are voiceless, whose voices need to be heard."

—Malala, after learning she had received the Nobel Peace Prize

Oli Scarff / AFP

37

Malala, Her People, and Her Country

Malala wasn't even twelve years old when she made her first public declarations defending girls' right to an education.

Véronique de Viguerie / Getty Images / AFP

• **July 12, 1997**
Malala Yousafzai is born in Mingora, Pakistan.

• **January–March 2009**
Encouraged by her school-director father, Malala writes a blog in the Urdu language that is published by the BBC under the pseudonym Gul Makai. The blog, titled *Diary of a Pakistani Schoolgirl*, denounces the Taliban's violent actions. She is only eleven years old.

• **February 2009**
Malala begins giving interviews and participating in conferences.

• **December 19, 2011**
Malala receives the first-ever National Youth Peace Prize, created by the Pakistani government. The prize is later renamed the National Malala Peace Prize. The award makes her a target of the Taliban.

• **October 9, 2012**
Malala is the victim of an assassination attempt on her way home from school. A bullet goes through her head and neck, and she almost dies.

• **October 15, 2012**
Malala is transferred from the Military Hospital Rawalpindi, Pakistan, to a hospital in Birmingham, England. All expenses are covered, although Malala worries about this.

• **December 10, 2012**
UNESCO (United Nations Educational, Scientific, and Cultural Organization) and Pakistan launch the Malala Fund for Girls' Right to Education, with the goal of helping girls gain access to education.

• **January 3, 2013**
Malala leaves the hospital, but she returns later to undergo another operation.

- **January 9, 2013**
Malala receives the Simone de Beauvoir Prize for Women's Freedom.

- **July 12, 2013**
Malala celebrates her sixteenth birthday by addressing the United Nations with a speech to promote education. The UN calls the day Malala Day.

- **September 17, 2013**
In Dublin, Ireland, Amnesty International awards Malala its most prestigious honor—the Ambassador of Conscience Award.

- **November 20, 2013**
Malala receives the European Parliament's Sakharov Prize for Freedom of Thought.

- **October 10, 2014**
Malala wins the Nobel Peace Prize.

Malala's Country, Pakistan

Today Malala lives in the United Kingdom due to death threats against her in her home country of Pakistan. Pakistan is an Islamic republic located on the Indian subcontinent. It gained independence from British rule on August 14, 1947, when British India was divided into Pakistan and India. Muhammad Ali Jinnah was the first governor-general. Pakistan has always had a difficult relationship with two neighboring countries, India and Afghanistan.

Pakistan has more than 190 million inhabitants. It is the sixth most populous country in the world. Though its capital is Islamabad, the largest city is Karachi, with more than twenty million inhabitants. The city of Mingora, where Malala used to live, is located north of Islamabad, in the Swat district. It has nearly 300,000 residents, most of whom are Pashtuns.

Urdu is the official language of Pakistan, but people also speak English, as well as the languages of different ethnic groups. One of those languages is Pashto, spoken in the area where Malala grew up.

Agriculture is the main economic sector in Pakistan.

Since the end of the 1990s, the northwest regions of Pakistan have suffered from Taliban attacks and from the military response of the Pakistani government. The relationship between the government and the Taliban is very complicated and changes often, even now.

The Pashtun People

There are many Pashtuns in Afghanistan. But the largest Pashtun population is in Pakistan. Pashtuns have strong traditions, immense pride, and unfailing hospitality. Pashtun people used to travel with their animal herds, but today many have settled in one place. Pashtun people speak Pashto, one of the two official languages of Afghanistan (the other is Dari).

In Pashtun culture, nobody forgives and forgets. Malala is convinced that education, rather than revenge, can settle conflicts.

Girls and School

The Alarming Situation for Girls in Pakistan

In Pakistan, most women have fewer rights than men, and many are victims of violent acts: sexual harassment, domestic isolation, arranged (sometimes forced) marriages, honor killings, and more.

Purdah (from Urdu and Persian, meaning "curtain") is still sometimes observed and requires women to cover their heads and bodies, stay at home, and not talk with men other than their family members.

According to UNESCO, less than 26 percent of girls in Pakistan know how to read and write. There are 163,000 primary schools in Pakistan, and fewer than 40,000 of them accept girls. Only seven million girls under the age of ten go to primary school (barely half); only three million go to high school; and fewer than 500,000 go to college or university. The situation is particularly serious in rural areas, mainly because of poverty.

Education in the World

According to UNESCO, about 475 million women worldwide are illiterate. Fifty-eight million children (nearly one in four) don't go to school. Twenty-eight million of those live in areas affected by conflict, and more than half are girls. Fifteen years after UNESCO's Education for All movement was renewed in 2000, only one-third of the 164 countries that signed the pact have achieved its objectives. Among the most underperforming countries are Pakistan, Yemen, and many in sub-Saharan Africa.

Young Pakistani girls at a school in Mingora.

A. Majeed / AFP

Isaac Babtunde / AFP

In April 2014, an Islamic extremist group called Boko Haram abducted 276 girls from a school in Chibok, Nigeria. Malala Yousafzai shows her support by meeting with girls who escaped and demanding that the rest be released.

Malala and Religion

In Multan, Pakistan, Islamic extremist militants burn the UN flag to protest Malala Yousafzai's Nobel Peace Prize.

S.S. Mirza / AFP

In October 2012, women demonstrate in the streets of Islamabad, shouting, "Shame on the Taliban!" in response to the attempt to assassinate Malala.

Aamir Qureshi / AFP

Like all Pashtuns and lots of Pakistanis, Malala is Muslim, a member of the Islamic faith. The Qur'an is the sacred book of her religion. She refuses fundamentalist applications of Islamic Sharia law (that regulates public and some private aspects of life) and denounces those who use Islam to take freedom away from women, children, and men.

She is opposed to terrorists who justify acts by saying, "It's God's will!" and to those who engage in jihad, or "holy war."

Malala believes that someone who has read the Qur'an should know that one should not kill. She challenges those who threaten to kill girls if they go to school. She points out that the Qur'an states that one must "seek knowledge, study passionately, and learn about the mysteries of the world." She challenges the prohibitions against women voting, and against people singing, dancing, getting vaccinated, and watching television. She disagrees with anyone who demands certain behaviors and those who kill in order to silence voices and intimidate people.

Malala's Inspiration

Malala often refers to important historical and humanitarian figures in her speeches. Pashtun people and culture have also shaped her way of thinking and acting.

Gul Makai

Malala took her pseudonym from Gul Makai, the heroine of a Pashtun folk story. In it, two teens fall in forbidden love—they are from different tribes. Their relationship causes a violent conflict. Gul Makai succeeds in convincing the elders that, according to the Qur'an, war is terrible. At the end of the story, the two tribes find peace and allow the lovers to unite.

Malalai

Malala was named after Malalai, the greatest Afghan heroine. In 1880 Malalai was assisting the injured on a battlefield where her father and her fiancé were fighting off the British. When the Afghans lost their flag bearer, Malalai waved her white veil and didn't hesitate to walk to the front of the battalion. A bullet struck and killed her. Her bravery inspired the soldiers, who went on to defeat the British.

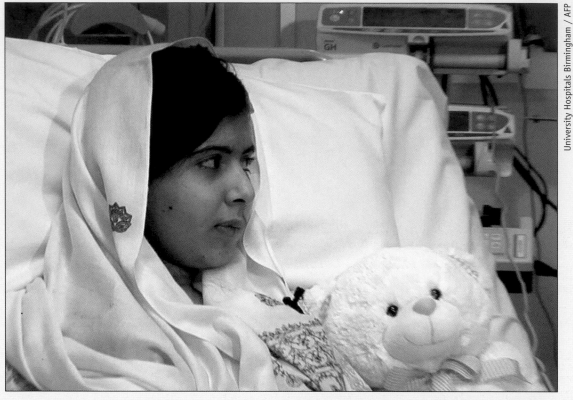

Malala receives messages of support and affection from around the world after she is transferred to a hospital in Birmingham, England.

University Hospitals Birmingham / AFP

Mahatma Gandhi

Mahatma Gandhi was born in India in 1869. He fought for his country's independence from Britain. He led a national campaign to help the poor, to fight for Indian women, and to end the social exclusion of people from the lowest caste or social status. While advocating for mass civil disobedience, he led many nonviolent activities for human dignity and justice, and he inspired many people. His work promoted solidarity between different religions and ethnic groups. Gandhi was assassinated in 1948.

Several months after the attempt on her life, Malala is able to continue her studies in England.

Liz Cave / AFP

Nelson Mandela

Nelson Mandela was born in South Africa in 1918. He was condemned to life in prison in 1964 because he fought apartheid, a political system of racial segregation that allowed severe discrimination against black people, even though they made up 90 percent of South Africa's population. Mandela was released in 1990 after twenty-seven years in prison. He negotiated with Frederik Willem de Klerk, the country's president, to abolish apartheid and give all South Africans the right to vote. In 1994 he became the first black president of South Africa. He championed national reconciliation among people of all races and fought against economic inequality and poverty. Mandela died in 2013, ten years after he received the Nobel Peace Prize.

Martin Luther King Jr.

Martin Luther King Jr. was born in 1929 in Atlanta, Georgia. At that time, there were laws separating black people from white people in many parts of the United States. There were black neighborhoods and white neighborhoods, separate schools, restaurants, and buses. King was a black Methodist pastor who fought for civil rights for black Americans. He carried out nonviolent acts of resistance against racist laws and fought against poverty. He dreamed of a world where freedom and justice existed for all. King was assassinated in 1968, four years after he received the Nobel Peace Prize.

The entire Yousafzai family, reunited in Birmingham, England.

The crowd cheers for Nobel Peace Prize winners Malala Yousafzai and Kailash Satyarthi, an Indian activist who fights against child labor, in Oslo, Norway, after the award ceremony.

Malala's Words

On her eighteenth birthday, Malala is in Lebanon with Syrian refugees to celebrate the opening of a school financed by the Malala Fund.

Rizwan Tabassum / AFP

"I want to tell other children all around the world that they should stand up for their rights. They should not wait for someone else, and their voices are more powerful."

"They thought that the bullets would silence us, but they failed. . . . Nothing changed in my life except this: weakness, fear, and hopelessness died. Strength, power, and courage was born."

"It does not matter what's the color of your skin, what language do you speak, what religion you believe in. It is that we should all consider each other as human beings and we should respect each other."

"Today we all know that education is our basic right. Not just in the West; Islam, too, has given us this right. Islam says every girl and every boy should go to school."

Young people in Karachi, Pakistan, celebrate Malala Day.

Malin Fezehal / AFP

"The extremists are afraid of books and pens."

"With guns you can kill terrorists; with education you can kill terrorism."

"If one man can destroy everything, why can't one girl change it?"

"Malala Day is not my day. Today is the day of every woman, every boy, and every girl who have raised their voice for their rights."

"We can fight against war through dialogue, peace, and education."

FOR MORE INFORMATION

Yousafzai, Malala, with Christina Lamb. *I Am Malala: The Girl Who Stood Up for Education and Was Shot by the Taliban.* New York: Little Brown, 2013.

———. *Diary of a Pakistani Schoolgirl* (blog), January–March 2009. http://news.bbc.co.uk/2/hi/south_asia/7834402.stm

The Malala Fund, www.malala.org.

Read the text of Malala's speech to the United Nations on July 12, 2013. www.independent.co.uk/news/world/asia/the-full-text-malala-yousafzai-delivers-defiant-riposte-to-taliban-militants-with-speech-to-the-un-8706606.html

Watch a video of Malala's speech to the United Nations on July 12, 2013. www.bbc.com/news/world-asia-23291897

Read the text of Malala's speech when she won the Nobel Peace Prize. www.nobelprize.org/nobel_prizes/peace/laureates/2014/yousafzai-lecture_en.html

Search for Malala's name in your favorite web browser.